The Global Phenomenon of K-Dramas: A Cultural Influence Transcending Borders

Introduction:

Korean dramas, colloquially known as K-Dramas, have carved a prominent niche in the global entertainment landscape, captivating audiences far beyond their country of origin.

With their intricate plots, compelling characters, and high production values, K-Dramas have emerged as a cultural force that transcends geographical boundaries.

This book delves into the profound influence of K-Dramas on popular culture, exploring their rise to prominence, key characteristics, and enduring impact on audiences worldwide.

Origins and Rise to Prominence

Korean television dramas have a rich history dating back to the 1960s, but it wasn't until the late 1990s and early 2000s that they gained international recognition.

One of the earliest breakthrough hits was "Winter Sonata" (2002), which captivated audiences across Asia and sparked the global K-Drama phenomenon.

Since then, K-Dramas have experienced exponential growth in popularity, fueled by factors such as improved production quality, innovative storytelling, and accessible streaming platforms.

Key Characteristics

Several distinctive characteristics contribute to the widespread appeal of K-Dramas.

First and foremost is their emphasis on storytelling. Many K-Dramas feature complex narratives that blend romance, drama, comedy, and suspense, keeping viewers engaged throughout multiple episodes. Moreover, K-Dramas often explore universal themes such as love, family, friendship, and societal issues, making them relatable to diverse audiences.

Another hallmark of K-Dramas is the depth and development of their characters.

Protagonists are typically multi-dimensional, flawed yet endearing individuals who undergo significant growth over the course of the series.

Audiences form deep emotional connections with these characters, rooting for their triumphs and empathizing with their struggles.

Furthermore, K-Dramas are renowned for their visually stunning cinematography and production values.

From picturesque filming locations to elaborate costumes and set designs, every aspect is meticulously crafted to create an immersive viewing experience.

Additionally, K-Dramas often incorporate elements of Korean culture, including traditional customs, cuisine, and language, providing audiences with a glimpse into Korean society and heritage.

Global Impact

The influence of K-Dramas extends far beyond entertainment, permeating various aspects of popular culture worldwide.

One significant impact is the exponential growth of Hallyu, or the Korean Wave, which refers to the global spread of Korean culture. K-Dramas serve as a flagship component of the Hallyu phenomenon, contributing to the increased interest in Korean music, fashion, cuisine, and tourism.

Moreover, K-Dramas have played a pivotal role in shaping global perceptions of South Korea.

Through their portrayal of modern Korean society, values, and traditions, these dramas have helped to challenge stereotypes and foster cross-cultural understanding.

As a result, South Korea has emerged as a cultural powerhouse, exerting soft power on the global stage.

The influence of K-Dramas is particularly evident in the realm of fashion and beauty. The stylish wardrobes and impeccable grooming of K-Drama actors have sparked fashion trends and influenced consumer preferences worldwide.

Korean beauty products, renowned for their innovation and quality, have also gained widespread popularity, with many consumers eager to replicate the flawless complexion of their favorite K-Drama stars.

Furthermore, K-Dramas have catalyzed the growth of the global streaming industry.

Platforms such as Netflix, Viki, and Rakuten Viki have capitalized on the immense popularity of K-Dramas by offering a wide selection of titles with multi-language subtitles.

This accessibility has made it easier for international audiences to discover and enjoy K-Dramas, further expanding their reach and influence.

The phenomenon of K-Dramas has also fostered vibrant online communities, where fans from around the world come together to discuss, analyze, and celebrate their favorite dramas.

Social media platforms, fan forums, and dedicated websites serve as virtual meeting places for enthusiasts to share their thoughts, fan art, and fan fiction, forging connections across cultural and linguistic barriers.

Conclusion:

In conclusion, K-Dramas have emerged as a global cultural phenomenon, captivating audiences with their compelling storytelling, rich characters, and high production values.

From their humble beginnings in South Korea, K-Dramas have transcended borders to become a ubiquitous presence in popular culture worldwide.

Through their influence on fashion, beauty, tourism, and digital media, K-Dramas continue to shape global trends and perceptions, leaving an indelible mark on the cultural landscape of the 21st century.

As the popularity of K-Dramas shows no signs of waning, their enduring impact on popular culture is poised to endure for years to come.

Please use the next few pages for your notes and debates.

www.ingramcontent.com/pod-product-compliance
Lightning Source LLC
Chambersburg PA
CBHW071001220526
45471CB00007B/3129